Out of the Hat

Children's Book of Magic

by

Brian Irwin

The Boyce Press

Santa Maria, CA

The Boyce Press
4869 S. Bradley #18B-208
Santa Maria, CA 93455
1-800-314-4556

Editor: Betty Boyce

Cover Design: Anne Whitten

Illustrations: Anna Rubcic

Printing: Nix Printing

Binding: Concord Spiral Bindery

ISBN# 1-892631-00-8
Printed in the United States of America

To my family and my friends,
for their never ending support
and motivation.
Especially to my wife, Lisa,
whose smile carries me through this magical
journey—life.

Author's Note

The tricks in *Out of the Hat, Children's Book of Magic* are a collection of public domain, historically performed magic. They include tricks submitted by children across the nation. These tricks are identified with the children's first names and grades. For submissions by more than one youngster of the same or similar tricks, the names of all who submitted are listed.

As the author/magician, I successfully performed each trick several times following the step-by-step instructions. However, I make no claim as to the successful performance of others, of any age, who follow the step-by-step instructions precisely. I further state that parental supervision is required for the safety of youngsters who perform the tricks.

Publisher's Note

The publisher, The Boyce Press, a division of Boyce Enterprises, does not assume responsibility for accuracy or origin of the tricks in this publication.

Table of Contents

Acknowledgments

Heartfelt thanks are extended to all the amazing youngsters and adults across the nation who continue to participate in the effort by passionately donating their time and talents in a myriad of ways to find a cure for Fibrodysplasia Ossificans Progressiva (FOP). Additional thanks go to those involved in this FOP research fundraiser, including those who submitted tricks—or even thought of submitting tricks—those who previewed tricks, those who collated all the pages for spiral binding, those who created the magic wands, and those involved in the ongoing process of marketing this publication, ***Out of the Hat, Children's Book of Magic.***

Foreward

Brian Irwin is good. He's real good! Brian appeared, materialized you might say, on my doorstep when he was a junior in high school. He was bright and very eager to learn.

Brian started coming to my home on a regular basis for lessons to learn everything he could from me about magic. In teaching magic to any new candidates, I would start them out with a trick that would be difficult enough to require some practice in order to perform it. When Brian came to me, he not only showed a vital interest, but when given the project he would work out the routine assigned and then add his own ideas and innovations. I knew then that he had the potential of becoming great.

Brian is a perfectionist, and his hands are trained to flawless dexterity. In his studies, Brian's quick mind absorbed the verbal coaching as well as the reading and retention of much of the literature on magic. Brian's fascination with CLOSE-UP magic is a natural outlet for his creative and innovative style. And he's fun. His genuine love for people shows in everything he does. Brian has become a master of CLOSE-UP. This mastery coupled with his quick energetic step, his contagious smile, and his happy sparkling eyes bring to his audience the sense of being his immediate friend.

During his years of training, Brian worked with me on stage and traveled with me. One of our experiences together was that of traveling to Colon, Michigan, where a Magicians' Convention was being held. With Brian as my assistant, we walked off with the Jack Gwynne Traveling Trophy for Excellence in Magic Award.

Brian has had fun with me too. I had taught him to "practice in front of a mirror until you can fool yourself." Now there have been many times that he has come to my home with a new trick that he has mastered to fool me! Then he will teach me his new trick.

Brian is comfortable on the large stage as well as doing small close-up work. His show is kept within the range of good family entertainment and pure enjoyment. It has been my great pleasure to have worked with Brian; and yes, I enjoy Brian Irwin.

Ralph Adams

Ralph Adams, Sr.

Introduction

There is magic in this book. It comes from children and is for children. The purpose of the book is to generate funds for medical research. The children who will benefit from the generosity of this magic have an uncommonly rare and devastating condition called Fibrodysplasia Ossificans Progressiva, or FOP.

FOP is a rare genetic disorder in which normal bone forms in abnormal locations, such as muscles, tendons, ligaments and other connective tissue. Bridges of extra bone form across the joints and lead to stiffness, locking and permanent immobility. Any attempt to remove the extra bone causes explosive new bone formation. Even minor bumps and bruises can cause a flare-up, which means that the body will produce extra bone at the site of the bump or bruise. In other words, FOP is a disease in which the body produces not just too much bone, but an extra skeleton that immobilizes the joints of the body and completely restricts movement. People who have FOP are imprisoned in their body by an extra skeleton. The goal of medical research is to determine the genetic cause of FOP and to use that information to devise a cure (a sort of skeleton key) that will release the children from their prisons of bone.

We live in a complex and mysterious world. When we see pleasant and surprising things that we cannot explain—things that seemingly defy the reality we expect—we call that *magic*. But there is often a deeper reality behind magic, a reality that simply eludes our perceptions. Magic usually means that we are not seeing the whole picture. The magician knows something we do not, and we are eager to ask, "How did you do that?" Often, when we learn the "trick" behind the magic, we are still surprised to see how our mind can make it seem otherwise. With FOP, we do not currently see the whole picture. That ignorance will hopefully be eliminated by medical research.

By finding the damaged gene that causes FOP, we will be able to devise more effective medications to treat the condition and eventually cure it. There is nothing magic about that at all, but if that can be done, it will seem like magic to children whose joints are catastrophically frozen with extra bone. Our goal is to use this book of magic to generate funds for medical research to bring real magic to children whose lives desperately depend on it.

By Frederick S. Kaplan, M.D.
Isaac and Rose Nassau Professor of Orthopaedic Molecular Medicine and
  Chief of the Division of Metabolic Bone Diseases and Molecular Orthopaedics
The University of Pennsylvania School of Medicine
  Dr. Kaplan, is co-director of the FOP laboratory located at the University of Pennsylvania and is medical advisor to the International FOP Association.

The Journey Begins . . .

How it Works

About the Tricks

Each trick follows the same routine:
- *Preview* is a sneak peek of the trick.
- *Requirements* is a list of all the items needed for the trick.
- *Preparation* describes all the details that must be done in advance and out of view of the audience.
- *Do the Trick* is a step-by-step description of how to do the trick.
- Many of the tricks include *Brian's Bonus,* which expands on the concept of the trick.
- Within the tricks, Glossary terms are in ***bold italic***. If you don't understand a term, go to the Glossary to learn the definition.

Here's How to Learn Tricks

1. Read through the entire trick. *Imagine* you were seeing it performed.
2. Read the trick a second time while you visualize how the trick is done. Close your eyes and "see" it.
3. Gather all items (props) you need for the trick. Review how each prop is used.
4. In front of a mirror, read and follow the instructions exactly. When a prop is introduced, hold it the right way, in the correct hand, palm up or palm down. It doesn't matter if you are right- or left-handed. At first do the trick using the correct hand. Later you can experiment switching to your other hand. The important factor is to get both hands functioning. If you get mixed up, just look in the mirror, smile, and start over.
5. When you are able to get all the way through the trick, immediately do it again and again.
6. Continue reading the instructions until you can remember the steps without looking.

WOW! You are on your way. Congratulations for making it through!

Once you have discovered what is most comfortable for you, continue to practice in front of a mirror until you can perform the entire trick without thinking about it. Practice until you feel it flowing naturally. Have Fun. Celebrate each new trick by performing it for your family and friends.

———————————————— A note from Brian

I follow these steps when I learn new tricks. By following the steps, you will find that learning a new trick is easy. You will learn not only how a trick works, but why.

Good luck as you take the steps on your Magical Journey.

Brian Irwin

Practice Makes Perfect

Perfect practice gives perfect results. Review each step carefully when you practice a move or trick so you do not develop any bad habits. If you want to entertain people with your magic you must practice! You must be able to do all moves smoothly and confidently. Practice in front of mirror until you can fool yourself. If you cannot perform perfectly for the mirror, you will not do well in front of an audience. You *must never* perform a trick for anyone *ever* without properly preparing. Make sure that when you practice your magic, you follow the directions exactly. *Never* let yourself skip a step. Each step is there for a reason.

Putting it all Together

After you learn a few tricks, it's time to combine three or four of them into a smooth-flowing routine. In selecting tricks for your routine, include ones that got the best responses when you performed them. This way you know that you will be combining your strongest tricks *from the spectator point of view*. This will give you a powerful and entertaining routine.

As you begin to develop a routine, pick an opening trick that will really get the attention of your audience. Next, include a trick where you can let them relax. You may want the second trick to be a participation trick. At this point, you become their friend. Maybe halfway through your routine something goes wrong and you messed up. The audience loves it when the magician seems to mess up. Of course, the trick ends just fine. Now you really have their attention because they think you almost flubbed a trick—and they are watching you closely. This is a great time for the grand finale. This is the trick they will be talking about when they go home. Be creative in the trick selection process. Remember you can always replace one trick with another.

As you progress through the development of your routine, try to blend. For example, use a card or coin from the first trick in the second trick, or try using a string or rope from the third trick to the fourth trick. Plan to develop several routines that you can perform.

Chapter 1

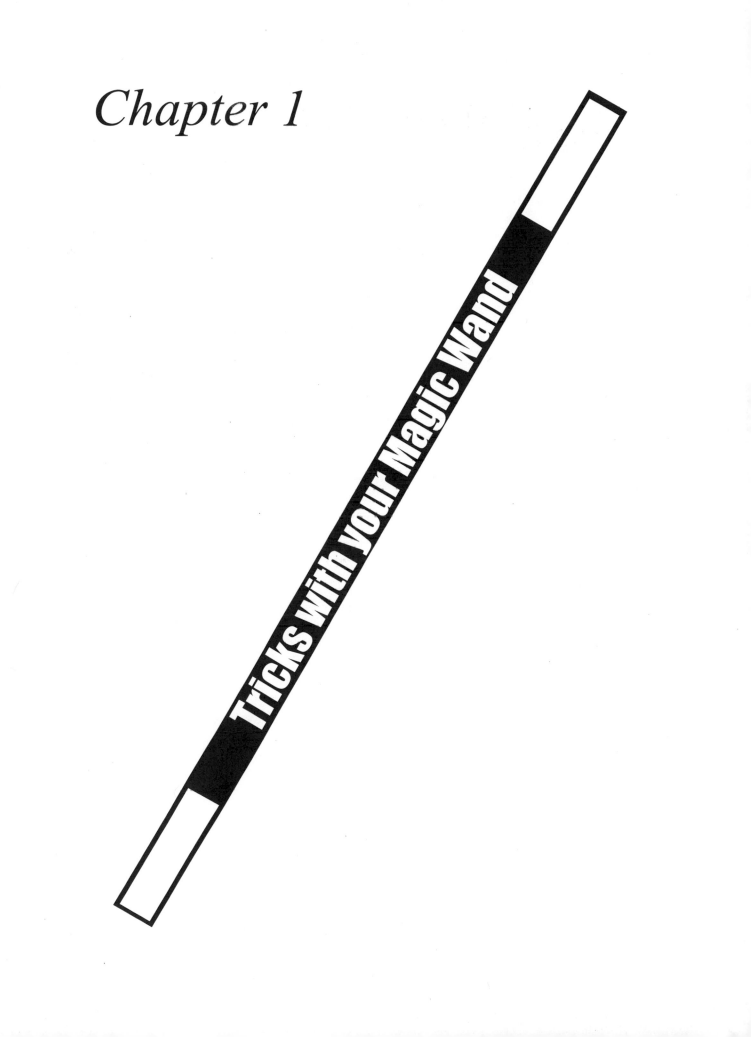

Tricks with your Magic Wand

Magic Notes

The Growing Magic Wand

Preview: A small magic wand grows up.

Items Needed: Your "Out of the Hat" Magic Wand, white paper, clear tape, scissors, and a ruler.

Preparation: Wrap and tape a piece of white paper (about 3/4 inch wide) around the plain end of your magic wand. Make sure the paper ring slides freely along the length of the wand. Slip the end of the wand with the streamers up your right sleeve (Fig 1).

Do the Trick:
Step 1. Hold the wand in your right hand so only about two inches can be seen.
Step 2. Wave your left hand in a magical pass, and take hold of the tip of the wand.
Step 3. Pull the wand out about two inches. Be sure to hold the paper ring with your right fingers so the wand slides through it (Fig. 2).
Step 4. Make another magical pass, and then pull the wand slowly until you reach the end.
Step 5. Now, simply hold the wand in your right hand so the paper ring cannot be seen.

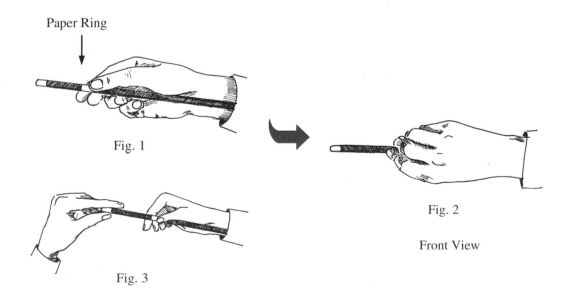

Paper Ring

Fig. 1

Fig. 2

Front View

Fig. 3

7

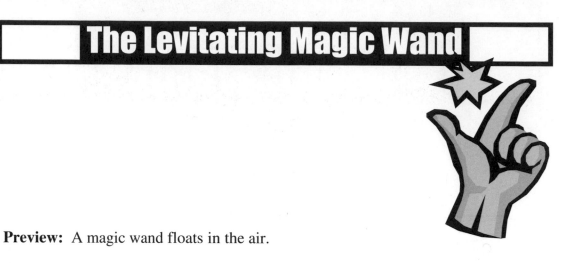

The Levitating Magic Wand

Preview: A magic wand floats in the air.

Items Needed: Your "Out of the Hat" Magic Wand.

Preparation: None.

Do the Trick:
Step 1. Hold your magic wand in your right hand. Wave it around showing it.
Step 2. Place your magic wand across the palm of your left hand.
Step 3. Immediately turn your left hand with the back toward the spectators. It appears that you are steadying your left hand with your right hand by holding the wrist. You are really holding the wand in place with your right index finger (Fig. 1).

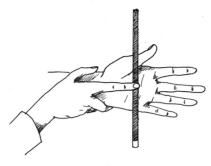

Fig. 1

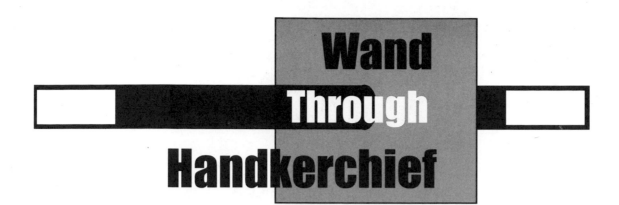

Wand Through Handkerchief

Preview: A wand goes through a handkerchief.

Requirements: Your "Out of the Hat" Magic Wand and a handkerchief.

Preparation: None.

Do the Trick:

Step 1. Place the handkerchief over your left fist. Center it covering your entire hand.

Step 2. Push your index finger into handkerchief to make a hole.

Step 3. Push the end of your wand into the hole far enough to hold it (Fig. 1).

Step 4. Turn your hand over to show there is no hole in the handkerchief.

Step 5. Remove wand from hole and begin again.

Step 6. Place the handkerchief over your left fist again, and make a hole with your index finger. This time, *use your second finger to create a second hole* on the outside of your left thumb (Fig. 2).

Step 7. Quickly press the wand down several inches in to the second hole. Reach below with your right hand, grab the wand *as though* it went through the handkerchief.

Step 8. Immediately shake out the handkerchief to show there is no hole.

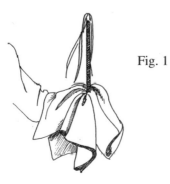
Fig. 1

Fig. 2

9

Rising Ring On Wand

Preview: A ring magically rises on your magic wand.

Requirements: Your "Out of the Hat" Magic Wand, a ring, clear tape, black thread, and scissors. Wear a dark colored shirt or blouse so the thread does not show.

Preparation: Cut a piece of black thread about 24 inches long. Tape one end of the thread to the plain end of your magic wand. Tape or loop the other end of the thread to a button on your shirt or blouse (Fig. 1).

Do the Trick:
Step 1. Borrow a ring, or use your own.
Step 2. Hold the wand with the streamers toward the floor.
Step 3. Slide the ring over the wand and thread until the ring is about three-fourths of the way down the wand.
Step 4. Hold the wand straight up in front of you (Fig. 2).
Step 5. Slowly move the wand away from your body. This tightens the thread, and the ring begins to rise. Remove the ring before it gets to the top of the wand.

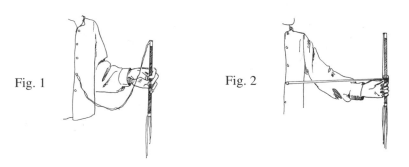

Fig. 1

Fig. 2

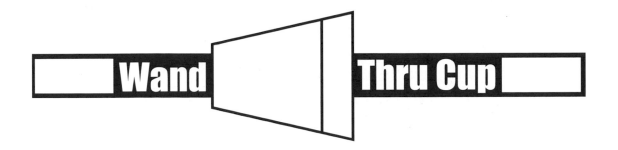

Wand Thru Cup

Preview: A magic wand goes through the bottom of a cup.

Requirements: A styrofoam cup and your "Out of the Hat" Magic Wand.

Preparation: None.

Do the Trick:
Step 1. Pick up the cup with your left hand. Show that it is empty.
Step 2. Pick up your magic wand with your right hand, holding it by the end with the streamers.
Step 3. With the top of the cup facing right, tap the inside bottom of the cup with the magic wand a few times. Then hold the wand out of the cup (Fig. 1).
Step 4. Now instead of tapping the inside bottom of the cup, slide the wand so it passes between your hand and the cup. It will look as though the wand passed through the bottom of the cup (Fig. 2).

Nick, Grade 4

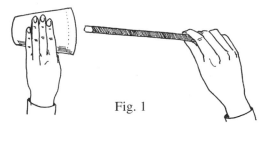

Fig. 1

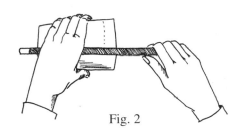

Fig. 2

Chapter 2

Magic Notes

Basic Coin Sleight-of-Hand

Coin magic can be one of the most rewarding types of magic that you will perform. When people find out that you are a magician, they will no doubt ask you to do a trick for them. It is easy to use a coin to amaze them with a miniature show.

It is very important that you practice your moves and routines until they become second nature to you. When you perform your coin magic within a few feet of your spectators, you need to be flawless. You must practice your moves in front of a mirror until you can fool yourself. You must watch yourself in a mirror from different angles as you perform. This makes you aware of the various views from which your audience is watching. You must practice until the moves become natural and you do not need to look at what you are doing.

You will soon notice that by practicing these moves with coins, you will be able to do these same moves with other small objects. These other objects could be small balls, marbles, or even sugar cubes. Being able to perform tricks with items other than coins will increase your hand dexterity and will add variety to your magic.

Look at your hands. Some people believe that their hands are too big or too small to perform *sleight-of-hand* magic. Don't worry whether you are right- or left-handed. With practice and watching your angles in a mirror, you will soon find ways to overcome any challenges you may encounter with your own hands. The moves you will learn are basic moves and can be modified and adjusted to whatever is comfortable to your hands.

Explore to discover which size coin works best for you. The size of the coin you use depends on what feels comfortable in your hand.

Look at a coin. Notice the little ridges around the edge. These ridges help you hold onto the coin when you place it into the position required for palming.

Good luck with your coin magic! Remember to practice, practice, practice!

The Classic Palm

Preview: Using the invisible "pocket" in the palm of your hand.

Requirements: A coin or other small object.

Preparation: Have coin in a convenient location.

Do the Trick:
Step 1. Hold the coin at the fingertips of your left hand.
Step 2. Place coin in the palm of the right hand (Fig. 1).
Step 3. Put your left hand, palm up, in front of you.
Step 4. Turn your right hand over onto your left, applying pressure to keep coin in the palm of your right hand. It looks as though you placed the coin in your left hand.
Step 5. Curl your left fingers upward.
Step 6. Move your right hand away with the coin still in it. Close your left hand as though the coin is in it (Fig. 2).
Step 7. With a slight upward toss, open your left hand. Coin appears to vanish.

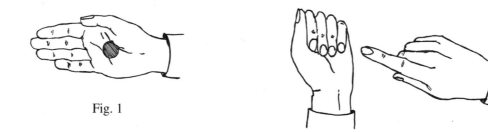

Fig. 1

Fig. 2

Brian's Bonus:
From the *vanish* (Step 7), curl your right fingers inward. Release pressure from the coin, dropping it to your finger tips or to right hand *finger palm* position. Reach behind your right knee. Put your thumb on the coin, pushing it forward, to make it reappear. It seems that you have just found the coin behind your right knee.

The Finger Palm

Preview: Use your fingers to hide a coin.

Requirements: A coin.

Preparation: Select several coins. Practice with each to decide which size is easiest to use.

Do the Trick:
Step 1. Hold the coin at the base of your second and third fingers.
Step 2. Curl your fingers inward slightly, applying pressure to the coin to hold it in position (Fig. 1). This is not really a trick in itself. It is a utility palm that you can use in a variety of tricks.

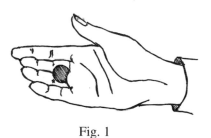

Fig. 1

Brian's Bonus #1: Practice pointing your index finger with the coin in *finger palm* position.

Brian's Bonus #2: Practice picking up your magic wand with the coin in **finger palm** position, then wave the wand over your other hand.

Brian's Bonus #3: When you are comfortable with this move using a coin, try using other small objects.

The Thumb Palm

Preview: A coin vanishes from your fingertips.

Requirements: A coin.

Preparation: None.

Do the Trick:
Step 1. Hold a coin between the tips of your first and second finger.
Step 2. Bend these fingers inward so the coin touches the base of your thumb.
Step 3. Position the coin so it is in the crotch of your thumb (Fig. 1).
Step 4. Apply pressure with your thumb so the coin stays in this flat position.

Fig. 1

The French Drop

Preview: Vanish a coin using the French drop.

Requirements: Your "Out of the Hat" Magic Wand and a coin. Practice the *finger palm*.

Preparation: Select the coin that is comfortable in your hand.

Do the Trick:
Step 1. Hold the coin by the edge with your left finger tips (Fig. 1).
Step 2. Pretend to take the coin with your right hand by smoothly bringing your right hand over the coin, fingers on top, and sliding your thumb under the coin (Fig. 2).
Step 3. Allow the coin to fall into left hand *finger palm* position, as your right hand turns away (Fig. 3).
Step 4. Close your right hand as though you have actually taken the coin.
Step 5. Pick up your magic wand with your left hand. Wave the magic wand over your right hand.
Step 6. Open your right hand to show that the coin has vanished. Celebrate!

Fig. 1

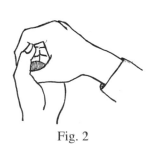

Fig. 2

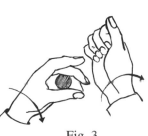

Fig. 3

Retention Vanish

Preview: A coin placed in your hand appears to *vanish*.

Requirements: A coin of any size.

Preparation: Have coin handy.

Do the Trick:
Step 1. Hold the coin in your right hand at the tips of your first two fingers and thumb. To aid in the *illusion*, leave as much of the coin visible as possible.
Step 2. Show the coin in this position (Fig.1).
Step 3. Put your left hand in front of you, palm up.
Step 4. Place the edge of the coin in the palm of the left hand (Fig.2).
Step 5. Curl the fingers of the left hand up to cover the coin (Fig.3). When the coin is out of the spectators' line of sight, push your right fingers down so the coin slides behind them.
Step 6. Pull your right hand away, dropping it to your side as you close your left fingers. (The coin is hidden in your right hand, and the spectators think it is in your left hand.)
Step 7. With an upward toss of your left hand, the coin appears to vanish.

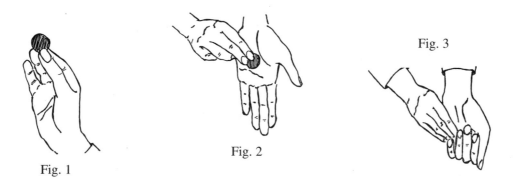

Fig. 1

Fig. 2

Fig. 3

Bria n's Bonus:
Be sure to work on the timing of curling your left fingers upward and pushing your right fingers downward over the coin. These two actions should be done at the same time.

Produce a Coin

Preview: A coin appears at your fingertips.

Requirements: A coin.

Preparation: Practice the thumb palm. Have the coin in thumb palm position (Fig. 1).

Do the Trick:
Step 1. Hold your hand with the back towards the audience.
Step 2. Bend your first and second fingers. Grab the coin with your fingertips.
Step 3. Quickly straighten your fingers with the coin at your fingertips.
Step 4. To make it more visible, grasp the coin with your thumb and fingers.

Christopher, Grade 5

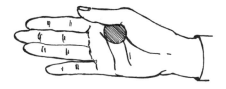

Fig. 1

Brian's Bonus:
This is also an excellent way to vanish a coin too. Notice that doing it backwards is the thumb palm vanish.

Invisible Coin

Preview: A coin appears.

Requirements: Double-stick tape and a coin.

Preparation: Use the double-stick tape to attach the coin to the back of your left hand. The coin stays taped to the back of your left hand throughout the trick.

Do the Trick:
Step 1. Show that the palms of your hands are empty. Say that you have an invisible coin.
Step 2. Pretend to flip an invisible coin into the air.
Step 3. As a diversion, ask a person to call heads or tails for how the coin will land.
Step 4. Pretend to catch the coin in your right hand.
Step 5. Immediately, put your right hand on the back of your left. Lift your right hand and the coin appears.
Step 6. Pretend to drop the coin from the back of left hand into the right hand and say "As fast as it appears, it disappears."

Kevin, Grade 6

Disappearing Coin

Preview: A coin *vanishes*.

Requirement: A coin.

Preparation: None.

Do the Trick:
Step 1. Place the coin in your right palm.
Step 2. Touch your left shoulder with your left hand.
Step 3. Rub the coin in your right hand on your left elbow.
Step 4. Accidentally drop the coin.
Step 5. Pick up the coin with your left hand.
Step 6. Pretend to place it in your right hand.
Step 7. Rub your right hand on left elbow. Your audience will think the coin is still in your right hand.
Step 8. Remove your hand from your elbow and Shazam! The coin has disappeared.
Step 9. Reach behind someone's ear with your left hand and produce the coin.

Danielle, Grade 4
Lauren, Grade 4

Disappearing Coin #2

Preview: A coin disappears.

Requirements: A pencil and a quarter.

Preparation: Place a pencil and a quarter on the table. Wear slacks with pockets.

Do the Trick:

Step 1. Pick up the coin. Put it in your left hand and close your hand.

Step 2. Pick up the pencil and tap your hand three times.

Step 3. Turn to the left and put the pencil behind your right ear.

Step 4. Say "Where's the pencil?" Coach the audience to tell you it is behind your ear. As they say this, you slip the coin into your left pocket.

Step 5. Face the audience, and open your left hand. The coin has vanished.

Step 6. Turn back to the left. Reach for the pencil with your right hand. Secretly remove the coin from your left pocket.

Step 7. Face the audience. Tap your right hand three times with the pencil. Open your hand. Magically the coin reappears.

Diane, Grade 4

Dime & Penny Trick

Preview: The *Vanishing* Dime.

Requirements: A dime and a penny. You must be able to do the ***thumb palm.***

Preparation: None.

Do the Trick:

Step 1. For your audience to see, display the penny in your left palm.

Step 2. For your audience to see, display the dime in your right palm.

Step 3. Move your right hand as though you were placing the dime in your left hand along with the penny.

Step 4. Curl your left fingers as though you are taking the dime, but merely wedge the dime into right hand ***thumb palm*** position.

Step 5. Open your left hand to show that, magically, the dime has vanished.

Creepy Coin

Preview: A dime takes a walk.

Requirements: A table with a table cloth, a plastic glass, two quarters, and a dime.

Preparation: Arrange the other items on the table in front of you.

Do the Trick:
Step 1. Place the two quarters about three inches apart on the table.
Step 2. Place the dime centered between the two quarters.
Step 3. Place the glass, upside down, resting on the quarters. Adjust placement of quarters if necessary. The dime is under the glass.
Step 4. Ask a volunteer to remove the dime from beneath the glass without touching the glass or the quarters.
Step 5. When the volunteer fails, simply scratch your finger nail on the table cloth. The dime will come to you.

Leonardo, Grade 4

I "Red" Your Mind

Preview: Determine which hand hides a coin.

Requirements: A chair, table, and a coin.

Preparation: Put the coin on the table. Place the chair nearby.

Do the Trick:
Step 1. Tell your audience you can determine which hand a volunteer will use to hold a coin.
Step 2. Select a volunteer. Ask that person to sit on the chair and place both hands on knees.
Step 3. Turn your back.
Step 4. Tell the volunteer to pick up the coin with either hand, hold it up to the light, and gaze at it. You count to seven slowly in your head.
Step 5. Tell the volunteer to return that hand to the knee, keeping the coin under it.
Step 6. Turn around. Look closely at both hands. The hand with the coin will be whiter because all the blood has run from it while the volunteer was gazing at the coin. Select this hand.

Paper Bag Trick

Preview: It is in the bag!

Requirements: A small paper bag.

Preparation: Practice holding an open paper bag while snapping your finger
against it (Fig. 1).

Do the Trick:
Step 1. Hold the open paper bag with your left hand. Note that the bag opens away
from your body.
Step 2. Toss an imaginary ball into the air.
Step 3. Pretend to catch it in the bag as you snap your finger against the bag. It will
sound like an object really landed in the bag.

Lyndsy, Grade 9

Brian's Bonus 1:
Step 1. Have an item already in the bag, such as a ball. Do not let your audience
know that anything is in the bag.
Step 2. Show your right hand and say that you have an invisible ball. Toss it into
the air and magically catch it in the bag.
Step 3. Reach inside the bag to pull out the real thing.

Brian's Bonus 2:
Step 1. *Conceal* four coins in left *finger palm* position (Fig. 2).
Step 2. Left fingers press coins against thumb through the bag (Fig. 3).
Step 3. Show an invisible coin in your right hand.
Step 4. Pretend to toss it into the air, following it with your eyes for effect.
Step 5. Release pressure of your thumb slightly to drop first coin in bag.
Step 6. Repeat with the remaining coins. Be creative with the imaginary path each
coin travels on way to the bag.
Step 7. Pour the coins into your right hand to display. Take a bow.

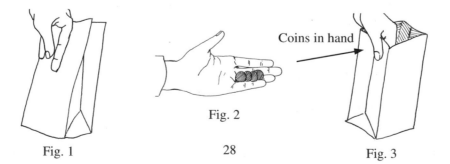

Fig. 1

Coins in hand

Fig. 2

Fig. 3

Upside-down George

Preview: A dollar bill flips over.

Requirements: A dollar bill.

Preparation: None.

Do the Trick:
Step 1. Hold the dollar bill in front of you with George Washington facing your audience.
Step 2. Fold the bill in half from right to left.
Step 3. Fold the bill down toward you.
Step 4. Open the front fold from the bottom to the top.
Step 5. Open the front fold from left to right. The bill is upside down.
Step 6. From the upside down position, repeat the steps to get bill right side up again.

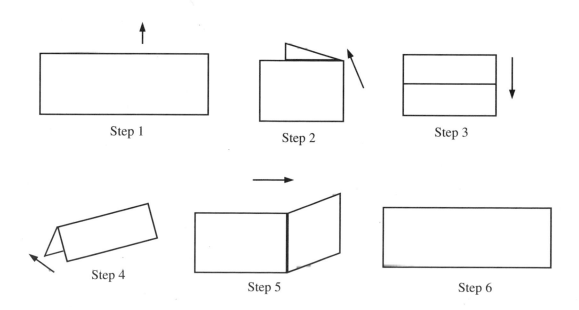

Step 1   Step 2   Step 3

Step 4   Step 5   Step 6

Linking Paper Clips

Preview: Paper clips magically link.

Requirement: Two paper clips and a dollar bill.

Preparation: None.

Do the Trick:
Step 1.   Hold the bill so George Washington is facing you.
Step 2.   Fold the right side of the bill 1/3 over to cover George Washington.
Step 3.   Place paper clip at the top over the front two parts (Fig. 1).
Step 4.   Fold the left side of the dollar bill behind George Washington. The dollar
　　　　　is folded in thirds.
Step 5.   Insert second paper clip over the back two parts (Fig. 2).
Step 6.   Hold the dollar bill by the edges and pull quickly. The paper clips will
　　　　　link together in mid air.

Cody, Grade K

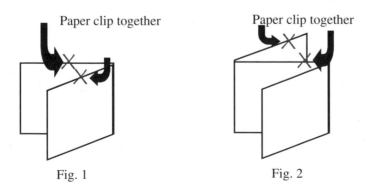

Fig. 1　　　　　　　　　　　　Fig. 2

Disappearing Quarter

Preview: A quarter *vanishes*.

Requirements: A small rubber band, a quarter, and a handkerchief.

Preparation: Place the rubber band around two fingers.

Do the Trick:
Step 1. Place the handkerchief over the hand that has the rubber band on the two fingers.
Step 2. With a finger of your other hand, push a hole down into the rubber band.
Step 3. Show a quarter and place it into the hole in the handkerchief.
Step 4. Slide the rubber band off your fingers, trapping the quarter in the small hole.
Step 5. Quickly swish the handkerchief through the air. It looks like the quarter has vanished.

Jessy, Grade 1
Chelsea, Grade 1
Mathew, Grade 5

Chapter 3

Rubber Bands, String and Rope

Magic Notes

Preston's "PRESTO" String

Preview: Cutting and *restoring* a string.

Requirements: A straw, scissors, and a 2-foot string.

Preparation: With the scissors, make a slit about four inches long in the center of the straw (Fig. 1).

Do the Trick:
Step 1. Show the audience the piece of string and the straw (with the slit facing you).
Step 2. Thread the string through the straw. Be sure string hangs out of both ends.
Step 3. Bend the straw in half with the slit downward, secretly pull the ends of the string down gently (Fig. 2).
Step 4. Ask a volunteer to cut the straw at the bend.
Step 5. After the cut, pull the straw apart showing that the string is not cut. Bravo!

Preston, Grade 1

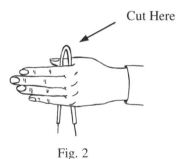

Cut Here

Fig. 1

Fig. 2

Jumping Rubber Band

Preview: A rubber band gets confused.

Requirements: A small rubber band.

Preparation: None.

Do the Trick:
Step 1. Place the rubber band around the index and middle fingers of your right hand (Fig. 1).
Step 2. Make a fist and show the audience your hand. As your fist closes, pull the rubber band back and to the left with your left hand (Fig. 2). Insert four right fingers inside the loop (Fig. 3).
Step 3. Let go of rubber band with the left hand. Count to three and open your hand. The rubber band has jumped to your ring and pinky fingers (Fig. 4).

Mikey, Grade 1
Caitlyn, Grade 2
Jonathan, Grade 4

Fig. 1

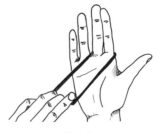

Fig. 2

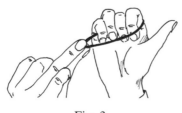

Fig. 3

Fig. 4

Two Strings to One

Preview: Two pieces of string magically become one.

Requirements: String and scissors.

Preparation: Measure and cut one 12-inch piece of string and one piece about 1½ inches long. Fold each string in the middle, and hold on the fold (Fig. 1).

Do the Trick:
Step 1. Show the pieces of string according to Figure 1.
Step 2. Put both pieces in your mouth, and begin to chew.
Step 3. Without letting your audience know, separate the smaller piece in your mouth and place it between your cheek and your gum with your tongue.
Step 4. Grasp an end of the long string with your fingers. Slowly remove it from your mouth. It appears that the pieces of string have become one.

Fig. 1

12 inch long piece   1 1/2 inch short piece

Rising Rubber Band

Preview: A rubber band rises on another.

Requirements: Two rubber bands.

Preparation: None.

Do the Trick:

Step 1. Pick up the first rubber band with your right hand. Hold it so about half of the length is hidden in your hand (Fig. 1).

Step 2. Pick up the second rubber band with your left hand. Hang it on the first one (Fig. 2).

Step 3. Grab the first rubber band with your left fingers, stretching it out and slightly upward. Keep the extra length hidden in right hand. Be sure the second rubber band is by your right fingers (Fig. 3).

Step 4. Slowly release the tension on the extra length of rubber band in your right hand. This movement is undetectable to the spectators. It looks like the first rubber band is sliding up the other one.

Mandi, Grade 3

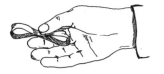

Fig. 1

Fig. 2

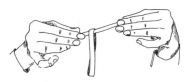

Fig. 3

Appearing Knot

Preview: A knot appears in a rope.

Requirements: A piece of rope about three feet long.

Preparation: Tie a knot in one end of the rope about four inches from the end. Hold rope so the knot is *concealed* in your right hand.

Do the Trick:
Step 1. Wave the rope around in front of you (Fig. 1).
Step 2. Tell everyone that you can tie the "fastest knot in the west."
Step 3. Grab the other end of the rope with your left hand and bring both hands together.
Step 4. With a snapping motion, quickly pull your left hand away from your right hand. Let go of the rope with your right hand. Tah-dah! A knot has magically appeared.

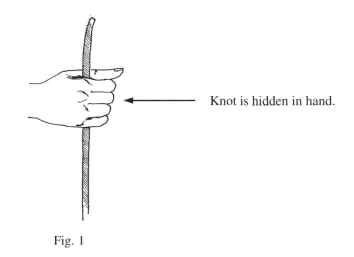

Knot is hidden in hand.

Fig. 1

Floating Ping Pong Ball

Preview: A ping pong ball floats from hand to hand.

Requirements: Black thread, scissors, a ruler, and a ping pong ball. Wear a dark colored shirt or blouse to hide the thread.

Preparation: Measure and cut a piece of thread about 24 inches long. Tie the ends of the thread, forming a loop. Stretch the loop of thread between your fingers. Perform the trick with your audience in front of you so your blouse or shirt hides the black thread.

Do the Trick:
Step 1. Toss the ping pong ball to spectators for examination.
Step 2. Take the ball back, and slowly separate your hands to tighten the thread.
Step 3. Place the ping pong ball onto the double thread track to support the ball (Fig. 1).
Step 4. Slightly tilt your hands from the left to the right to make the ball roll (float) between your hands. Your dark colored shirt or blouse hides the thread.

Fig. 1

Chapter 4

CARD

MAGIC

Magic Notes

Card Prediction

Preview: Predict the location of a card with a roll of dice.

Requirements: A deck of cards, two dice, a pencil, and a piece of paper.

Preparation: Count down to the 14th card of the deck. This card will be your prediction.

Do the Trick:

Step 1. Place the deck of cards, face down, in front of you on the table.

Step 2. Tell your audience you are going to write your prediction according to a roll of the dice.

Step 3. Write your prediction, the 14th card, on the piece of paper so your audience can't see it.

Step 4. Fold the paper, and give it to one of the spectators to hold.

Step 5. Select a spectator to roll the dice.

Step 6. Ask that person to add the top two numbers to the bottom two numbers of the dice. Note: these numbers will always equal 14.

Step 7. Hand the deck of cards to another spectator. Tell this person to deal the cards, face down, up to the 14th card; then turn the 14th card face up.

Step 8. Ask the person holding the paper to read your prediction. Take a bow!

Chris, Grade 4

Brian's Bonus:

Consider doing this trick with colors, or words, or even with letters. Experiment with your own ideas. This will work well to predict a number that relates to adding the top and bottom numbers of the roll of two dice.

Now You See It
Now You Don't!

Preview: A card *vanishes*.

Requirements: One card.

Preparation: None.

Do the Trick:
Step 1. Make your hand into a fist.
Step 2. Put the card in front of your two middle fingers and between your index finger and your pinky (Fig. 1).
Step 3. Wave the card up and down.
Step 4. In one smooth movement, open your hand. The card appears to have *vanished*.
Step 5. Quickly close your hand back into a fist, revealing the card once again.
Step 6. Watch the amazement on the faces of your audience!

Adam, Grade 9

Fig. 1

FIND YOUR CARD

Preview: An easy-to-do card location.

Requirements: A deck of playing cards.

Preparation: Separate the deck of cards into two stacks—red cards in one and the black in the other.

Do the Trick:
Step 1. Place both stacks of cards face down and side by side on the table.
Step 2. Invite a spectator to pick the top card from one of the stacks.
Step 3. Ask the spectator to look at the card, remember it, and place it anywhere face down in the other stack (without looking at the other cards in the stack).
Step 4. Pick up the stack in which the card was placed.
Step 5. Hold the cards facing you so the audience can see only the backs of the cards. With them facing you, fan the cards. Remove the card of the opposite color.
Step 6. Show it to the audience saying that it was the selected card.

Sarah, Grade 7
Christelle, Grade 4

Red and Black

Preview: The color of the card.

Requirements: A deck of cards.

Preparation: Separate the cards into two stacks with one stack of red cards and the other stack of black cards.

Do the Trick:
Step 1. Place the two stacks of cards face down on the table.
Step 2. Ask a spectator to select a stack and hand it to you.
Step 3. You fan the cards, face down.
Step 4. Ask the spectator to pick a card, show it to the other spectators, and remember the card. While this is happening, put the cards in your hand to one side and pick up the other stack. Casually do this so the spectators do not notice what you are doing.
Step 5. Tell the spectator to put the selected card anywhere in the stack.
Step 6. Shuffle the cards and fan them facing you (so the spectators cannot see the front of the cards).
Step 7. Select and show the card that doesn't match the color of the others. Enjoy the applause.

Clare, Grade 4
Christelle, Grade 4

The Secret Card Trick

Preview: Finding a card . . . with a twist.

Requirements: A deck of playing cards.

Preparation: Flip the bottom card of the deck so it is facing the other cards. This makes the bottom of the deck look like the top.

Do the Trick:
Step 1. Select a spectator.
Step 2. Fan the deck of cards from hand to hand. Be careful not to show that the bottom card is face up.
Step 3. Ask the selected person to pick a card and remember it.
Step 4. Ask the person to show the card to the other spectators.
Step 5. While the card is being shown, close the deck and flip it over. It will look as though the cards are facing down. However, only the top card is facing down.
Step 6. Ask the spectator to push the selected card back into the deck. Be careful not to show that the deck is really upside down.
Step 7. Put the deck behind you, flip the bottom card over so it is right side up.
Step 8. Bring the deck back in front of you.
Step 9. Fan the cards from one hand to the other. All the cards are face down except the spectator's card. Remove that card, and take your well deserved bow.

Matt, Grade 6
Justin, Grade 4

The Key Card

Preview: Locating a card in a ***shuffled*** deck.

Requirements: A deck of cards.

Preparation: Once the deck is ***shuffled***, glance at the bottom card of the deck and remember it. This is the ***key card***.

Do the Trick:
Step 1.   Spread the cards between your hands. Ask a volunteer to select a card, show it to the audience, and remember it.
Step 2.   Ask the volunteer to place the card face down on top of the deck.
Step 3.   Have the volunteer cut the deck, placing the bottom half on the top (the card you glanced at is now on top of the selected card).
Step 4.   Take one card at a time from the top of the deck, dropping each one face up on the table.
Step 5.   Once you flip over the ***key card*** flipped over on the table, say "Stop." Point to the card on top of the deck and say, "This is your card."
Step 6.   Ask the volunteer to show the card, and wow, you are right!

Jessica, Grade 11

False Shuffle

Preview: A selected card remains on top of the deck.

Requirements: A deck of cards.

Preparation: None.

Do the Trick:

Step 1. Remove the deck from the card case and *shuffle* the cards.

Step 2. Spread the cards face down between your hands. Ask a volunteer to select a card, remember it, and show it to the audience.

Step 3. Tell the volunteer to replace the card on top of the deck.

Step 4. Hold the deck of cards by the ends with your right hand thumb and fingers. Be sure the bottom card of the deck is facing the audience.

Step 5. With your left hand, grasp the center of the deck. Your thumb is on the bottom card and your fingers are on top (Fig. 1).

Step 6. With your right hand, pull only the center portion of the deck upward, holding the top and bottom cards with your left hand (this keeps the selected card in place). Pull this portion out of the deck (Fig. 2).

Step 7. This center of the deck is now *shuffled* onto the cards facing the audience in your left hand. Repeat this 1 or 2 more times.

Step 8. Turn the deck face down. Turn over the top card, showing the selected card. Enjoy the applause!

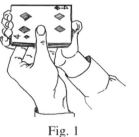

Fig. 1

Fig. 2

Brian's Bonus:
Put jazz into your performance before you come to Step 8. You may ask the person selected to push an imaginary elevator button on top of the deck. Say that when the elevator button is pushed, the selected card boards the elevator to bring it to the top of the deck.

The Rising Card

Preview: A selected card rises from a card box.

Requirements: A deck of cards.

Preparation: Practice the false shuffle—you must know it for this trick. Cut an opening into the back of the cardbox, flapside (Fig. 1). Make the cut 1 inch across by 2 ½ inches, starting at the bottom of the box.

Do the Trick:

Step 1. With the cards in the box, hold the box so the opening is towards the floor or facing you.

Step 2. Remove the cards from the box. Place the box down so the opening cannot be seen.

Step 3. Spread the cards, face down, on the table in front of you. Have someone select a card, remember it, and return it to the top of the deck.

Step 4. Hold the deck of cards by the ends with your right thumb and two fingers. Be sure the bottom card of the deck is facing the audience.

Step 5. Perform the false shuffle.

Step 6. Pick up the card box with your right hand. Be sure the opening is facing the palm of your hand.

Step 7. Slide the cards in the box. Be sure the selected card is against the opening. Do not close the lid.

Step 8. Position your right index finger on the selected card through the opening (Fig. 2).

Step 9. Make a magical pass over the card box with your left hand. Begin pushing upward on the selected card. Magically the selected card rises from the card box.

Brian's Bonus:

Be sure that you are confident with the false shuffle before performing this trick. With practice you will be able to push the card upwards so that no movement of your hand can be seen. Have fun with this one.

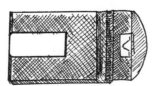

Fig. 1

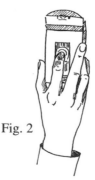

Fig. 2

The Rising Card #2

Preview: A selected card rises from the deck.

Requirements: A deck of cards.

Preparation: You must know how to do the false shuffle.

Do the Trick:
Step 1. Have someone select a card from the deck and remember it.
Step 2. Have the card returned to the top of the deck.
Step 3. Perform the false shuffle, keeping the selected card on top.
Step 4. Hold the deck of cards by the sides with your left hand. Cards face toward the audience (Fig. 1).
Step 5. Rub your right index finger on your left sleeve, pretending to create static electricity. Hold your finger about one inch above the deck. Move your finger up. Nothing happens (Fig. 2).
Step 6. Rub your finger on your sleeve again. As you put your index finger above the cards this time, extend your pinky so it touches the back of the card (Fig. 3). The spectators should not see you extend your pinky.
 Step 7. Slowly raise your hand. Apply pressure with your pinky to the back of the selected card. The card rises.

Fig. 1

Fig. 2

Fig. 3

Preview: Predict a card.

Requirements: A deck of playing cards, paper, pencil, and an envelope.

Preparation: Remove nine red cards and nine black cards from the deck. On the piece of paper, write "There will be two more black cards in the long row than red cards in the short row." Seal your prediction in the envelope.

Do the Trick:
Step 1. Tell your audience you have made a prediction. Place the sealed envelope on the table.
Step 2. Give the 18 cards to a volunteer. Ask the volunteer to shuffle the cards.
Step 3. Tell the volunteer to deal the cards, face up, in two rows in any order. Say that they must be arranged so that first row has seven cards and the second row has eleven cards.
Step 4. Remind your volunteer that the cards were dealt into each row by free choice.
Step 5. Open the prediction, you are correct.

Emily, Grade 4

The Floating Card

Preview: A card floats under your control.

Requirements: A deck of cards and clear double-sided tape.

Preparation: Place a small piece of double-sided tape in the palm of your left hand.

Do the Trick:
Step 1.   Say "I am going to make this card float on the bottom of my hand."
Step 2.   Pick up one card from the deck and lay it on your left hand (be sure the tape touches it).
Step 3.   Slowly turn your hand over, and magically the card floats.

Cessily, Grade 5

Chapter 5

Silk Scarves
& Handkerchiefs

Magic Notes

KNOTTY HANDKERCHIEF

Preview: An impossible knot.

Requirements: A handkerchief or long scarf.

Preparation: Place the handkerchief on the table in front of you.

Do the Trick:
Step 1. Pick up the handkerchief, holding it at opposite ends.
Step 2. Twirl it like a rope.
Step 3. Lay it in front of you.
Step 4. Ask a volunteer to tie a knot in the center of the handkerchief without letting go of the ends. It is not possible.
Step 5. Say that you will tie a knot without letting go. Cross your arms (Fig. 1).
Step 6. Pick up one end of the handkerchief with each hand (Fig. 2).
Step 7. Now, uncross your arms holding the ends tightly. A knot will appear in the center of the handkerchief.

Kevin, Grade 3

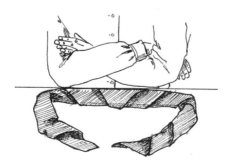

Fig. 1

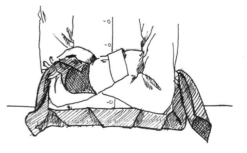

Fig. 2

Preview: A small scarf disappears.

Requirements: A plastic thumb tip and a small scarf.

Preparation: Place the thumb tip on your right thumb. Wear slacks or jeans with pockets.

Do the Trick:

Step 1. Reach into your right pocket, and remove the scarf.

Step 2. Wave the scarf around, showing it to the audience. Be sure your thumb with the thumb tip is behind the scarf (Fig. 1).

Step 3. Show your left hand empty and as you begin to push the silk into your hand. You secretly place the thumb tip in first (Fig. 2).

Step 4. Push the scarf into the thumb tip, completely out of sight (Fig. 3). Secretly push your right thumb into the thumb tip. Move your right hand away from your left, keeping the thumb tip hidden. Keep your left hand closed as though it contains the scarf.

Step 5. Make a magical pass over your left hand with your right hand. Open your left hand. The scarf has disappeared. Put your right hand in your pocket to get rid of the thumb tip and the scarf.

Brian, Grade 5

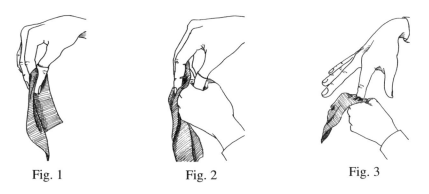

Fig. 1   Fig. 2   Fig. 3

Brian's Bonus:

As you finish this trick by placing your right hand into your pocket, pull the scarf from your pocket. With your left hand, press against the thumb tip through your slacks so the thumb tip does not accidentally come out with the scarf.

TRAVELING THIMBLE

Preview: A thimble takes a walk.

Requirements: Two thimbles and a handkerchief.

Preparation: Nest the thimbles together and place them on the index finger of
your right hand.

Do the Trick:
Step 1. Show the thimble (really two) on your finger.
Step 2. Drape the handkerchief over the thimbles.
Step 3. Reach under with your left hand and remove one thimble.
Step 4. Put it on the outside of the handkerchief, over the hidden thimble.
Step 5. Gather the corners of the handkerchief with your left hand. Quickly move
the handkerchief away. Be careful not to drop the thimble that is in the
scarf. Magic! The thimble is still on your finger.

DISAPPEARING PENCIL

Preview: A pencil disappears under a handkerchief.

Requirements: A pencil and a handkerchief. Wear a shirt or blouse with long sleeves.

Preparation: None.

Do the Trick:
Step 1. Hold the pencil, eraser up, in your right hand.
Step 2. Place the handkerchief over the pencil so it hangs down covering your hand.
Step 3. While positioning the handkerchief, extend your forefinger, making it appear to be the pencil. At the same time, slide the pencil into your sleeve.
Step 4. Make an upward tossing motion with your right hand, releasing the handkerchief into the air. The pencil has *vanished*. Take a bow.

Chapter 6

Miscellaneous
Mysteries

Disappearing Salt Shaker

Preview: A salt shaker takes leave.

Requirements: A paper towel, a salt shaker, and a penny.

Preparation: Arrange all the items on the table in front of you. You must be seated at the table.

Do the Trick:

Step 1. Place the penny on the table in front of you. Tell your spectators you will make the penny disappear.

Step 2. Place the salt shaker on top of the penny.

Step 3. Now place the paper towel over the salt shaker, wrapping it tightly so it takes on the shape of the salt shaker (Fig 1).

Step 4. Say "Hocus Pocus" and lift the shaker and the paper towel off of the coin. The coin is still there. While everyone is looking at the coin, bring the shaker and towel to the edge of the table. Let the shaker fall into your lap (Fig. 2). The paper towel will keep the shape of the salt shaker.

Step 5. Gently replace the paper towel shape over the coin. Push down on the towel with your other hand. The salt shaker has magically disappeared from beneath the paper towel.

Christopher, Grade 6
Kalani, Grade 4
Adrian, Grade 4
Leigh, Grade 5

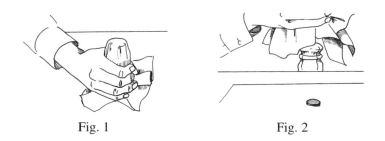

Fig. 1   Fig. 2

Brian's Bonus:
During Step #4 when the coin didn't disappear, you might say something like "the coin has to be heads up (or tails up)." Flip the coin accordingly. This puts more attention on the coin and keeps the spectators from seeing that you dropped the salt shaker in your lap.

Mesmerized Shaker

Preview: A salt shaker floats at fingertips.

Requirements: A toothpick and a salt shaker.

Preparation: Stand to perform. Have the toothpick in your right hand in *thumb palm* position.

Do the Trick:
Step 1. Position salt shaker on the table in front of you.
Step 2. Lower your right hand so your fingers touch the top of the salt shaker.
Step 3. Secretly push the toothpick into the middle holes. Be sure the toothpick is secure (Fig. 1).
Step 4. Slowly lift your hand, secretly holding onto the toothpick. The salt shaker appears to follow your fingers.
Step 5. Lower the shaker back to the table and secretly remove the toothpick.

Fig. 1

Cut & Restored

Preview: Cut and cut again.

Requirements: Classified section of the newspaper, rubber cement, scissors, and baby powder.

Preparation: Make up several of these at a time. Cut strips of classified ads out of the paper. Smoothly coat one entire side with a thin layer of rubber cement. Allow to dry for several hours. When dry, cover with the powder. The powder must cover all the cement. Shake loose powder off the paper. From a distance the paper should seem to be ordinary.

Do the Trick:
Step 1. Pick up a strip of paper and wave it around.
Step 2. Fold the strip in half with the rubber cement side inward (Fig. 1). The powder will keep the paper from sticking until the scissors cut and squeeze the rubber cement through the powder.
Step 3. Hold the strip at the open end with the fold down (Fig. 2).
Step 4. Cut off the fold about an inch from the bottom so everyone can see that you cut it.
Step 5. Pause for a moment, then let the strip fall open (the plain side must face the audience). Pause again while everyone sees that the cut is restored. Repeat as many times as you like, or until you run out of space.

Brian's Bonus:
This is fun because the audience actually sees you cut the paper several times. The cut paper is unmistakably on the floor. Yet, with your magical abilities, you are able to "heal" the cut. For variety perform this trick with music.

THREE TRICKY TUMBLERS

Preview: Do as I do!

Requirements: Three plastic glasses and a table. Note that tumblers also can be called glasses.

Preparation: None.

Do the Trick:

Step 1. On the table in front of you, place the center glass up and the other two glasses down (Fig. 1).

Step 2. Tell your audience to watch closely as you demonstrate how to turn the glasses in **three** moves so all will be upright. Say you will turn two glasses at a time and use a different hand to turn the glass for each step.

Step 3. Say, "One," as you flip the left and center glasses (Fig. 2).

Step 4. Say, "Two," as you cross your arms and turn the two outside glasses (Fig. 3).

Step 5. Say, "Three," as you turn the left and center glasses (Fig. 4). Note that all are upright. Take a bow.

Step 6. Casually, turn over the **center** glass. Invite a volunteer to perform the trick. Remind the volunteer to always change hands to turn over a glass. Tell the volunteer the steps: first turn the center and left glasses; second, cross your arms and turn the two outside glasses; and third, turn the left and center glasses. The volunteer will fail.

Stephanie, Grade 2

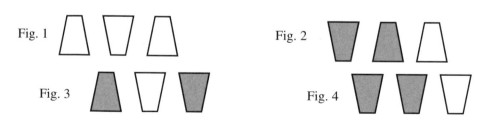

Brian's Bonus:

The reason the volunteer will fail is that you started with **the center glass up and the other two down**. The spectator started **with the center glass down and the other two up**. With this start, it is impossible to turn all three glasses up using these three moves.

Fearful Pepper Trick

Preview: This pepper's not all that hot.

Requirements: Medium bowl of water, black pepper, and liquid dish soap.

Preparation: Fill the bowl with water. Lightly coat your right index finger with soap.

Do the Trick:
Step 1. Place bowl of water on table in front of you. Tell the audience you can make the pepper move away from your finger.
Step 2. Sprinkle the water heavily with the black pepper.
Step 3. Let pepper stand for about 10 seconds.
Step 4. Put your right index finger into the peppered water. The pepper will rush to the sides of the bowl.

Cameron, Grade K

Preview: Make an object move with static electricity.

Requirements: A straw.

Preparation: Your spectators must be standing behind you or beside you.

Do the Trick:
Step 1. Place the straw on the table in front of you, and parallel to the edge of the table.
Step 2. Move your head about 10 inches from the straw.
Step 3. Say you will create static electricity to move the straw. Place your index finger on the table and circle the straw four times, then lift your finger.
Step 4. Reach over the straw to put your index finger on the table. Tell the spectators to watch closely while you move the straw.
Step 5. Leaning forward, blow gently on the straw as you drag your finger away (Fig. 1). It looks as though the straw follows your finger because of static electricity.

Christine, Grade 8

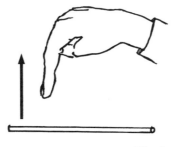

Fig. 1

Pick a Crayon

Preview: Color me Magic!

Requirements: Crayons.

Preparation: Practice rubbing the end of a crayon on your finger to determine how much pressure is needed to make a mark.

Do the Trick:
Step 1. Place the crayons on the table in front of you.
Step 2. Tell your audience that you will demonstrate that you can **feel** color.
Step 3. Select several volunteers, and ask each to take a crayon.
Step 4. Turn your back to the audience, and put your hands behind your back.
Step 5. Ask one of the volunteers to place a crayon in your hands.
Step 6. As you feel the crayon, rub the end against your index finger.
Step 7. Ask the volunteer to take back the crayon.
Step 8. Turn around, casually glancing at the crayon mark on your index finger.
Step 9. Announce the crayon color, and take a bow!

Desiree, Grade K

Brian's Bonus:
Try this. Instead of rubbing the crayon against your finger, scrape a tiny bit with your fingernail.

Floating EGG

Preview: Sunny side up.

Requirements: Two colored plastic glasses (that you cannot see through), one egg, salt, a spoon, and your "Out of the Hat" Magic Wand.

Preparation: Fill both plastic cups with water. With the spoon, dissolve one tablespoon of salt in one of the glasses of water.

Do the Trick:

Step 1. Have both glasses of water on the table. Tell your audience that you will make the egg float in one glass and sink in the other.

Step 2. Pass the egg for examination. Take egg back from the spectator. Wave your magic wand over the egg and say some magic gibberish.

Step 3. Place the egg into cup #1. It will quickly sink, then will rise and remain floating near the top.

Step 4. Remove the egg from cup #1 with the spoon and place it into cup #2. The egg sinks to the bottom and will remain there.

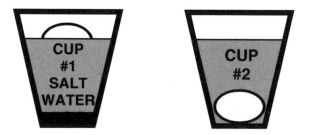

Brian's Bonus:

This is an experiment in *buoyancy*. The ability of a liquid to suspend an object. This is a great school experiment.

The Floating Paper Clip

Preview: A paper clip defies gravity.

Requirements: A full cup of water, one paper clip, a fork, a small amount of soap.

Preparation: The paper clips and cup need to be clean. Rub soap between the fingers and thumb of your left hand. Place the cup of water on the table.

Do the Trick:
Step 1. Point to the cup of water on the table and show the paper clip in your right hand.
Step 2. Tell your audience that you can float a paper clip and they can't.
Step 3. Place the paper clip flat on the fork. Slowly lower the paper clip into the water. When the paper clip begins to float, slowly remove the fork.
Step 4. With your soaped fingers, pick up the paper clip from the water. Hand it to a volunteer. Ask the volunteer to float it. The Paper clip will not work due to the soap. Soap breaks the surface tension of the water.

Caitlyn, Grade 2

Brian's Bonus:
This trick requires steady hands so that you do not submerge the paper clip in the water. Using the fork, place it lightly on the water. Beware if your audience wants you to do it again. You will need a clean cup of water and a clean paper clip because the soap has broken the surface tension of the water and will not hold the paper clip.

A Tight Squeeze

Preview: Fitting through a tight space.

Requirements: Piece of paper, a pencil, and a bicycle.

Preparation: None.

Do the Trick:
Step 1. Tell your friends that you can fit through the spokes of your bike.
Step 2. Write your name on the piece of paper and fold it so that it slips right through the spokes.

Monica, Grade 4

Chapter 7

Some Advanced
Tricks to Practice

Magic Notes

Three Choices
Three Choices
Three Choices

Preview: Predict a selected piece of paper.

Requirements: Three pieces of paper and a pencil.

Preparation: None.

Do the Trick:
Step 1. On one piece of paper write "You Will Choose This Paper." Do this so your spectators can't see what is written.
Step 2. Also out of spectators' view, write "Not This One" on the other two pieces of paper.
Step 3. Crumple the paper into three balls. *Remember* which one says "You Will Choose This Paper."
Step 4. Say "I will try to make you select a certain ball of paper. There will be a message to let you know if I am right or not."
Step 5. Ask a volunteer to pick up two of the balls of paper.
Step 6. If the volunteer picked up the two with "Not this one" on them, take the balls from volunteer. Tell the volunteer to pick up the ball remaining on the table and read it. It's the right one. If the ball with "You will choose this paper" is one they picked up, ask the volunteer to hand you a ball. You will be handed either the right one or the wrong one. If it is the right one, open it and read it out loud. If it's the wrong one, ask the volunteer to open the ball being held. It's the right one.

Brian's Bonus: A lot of what you say will be determined by the moves your volunteer makes. Do not rush this. You have plenty of time to keep track of the right ball during the whole routine.

A Self Self Levitation

Preview: Floating your body in the air.

Requirements: A large blanket. Note: you must be able to do a push-up.

Preparation: Practice doing push-ups, as described in this trick, until you can move smoothly and hold the position for at least 30 seconds.

Do the Trick:
Step 1. Lie on the floor face down.
Step 2. Cover yourself with the blanket from the neck down. The blanket should be centered with about 2 feet on each side of you. **Your feet must be covered.**
Step 3. Bring your hands under you at chest level. Balance your weight on your hands and your toes.
Step 4. Keep the leg closest to the spectators straight. Bend your other knee for balance, and slowly do a push-up with that leg (Fig. 1).
Step 5. Go as high as you can, keeping your body straight.
Step 6. Slowly lower yourself back to the floor.
Step 7. Remove the blanket, stand up, and take a bow.

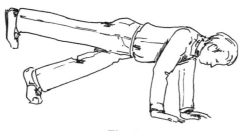

Fig. 1

Brian's Bonus
Do not rush this. When done properly, this is very powerful trick. Take the time to practice it. Your audience will love it.

Walk Through a Piece of Paper

Preview: It is all in the stretch.

Requirements: A piece of note book paper and scissors.

Preparation: Practice this a few times to get familiar with how the paper needs to be cut.

Do the Trick:
Step 1. Show the piece of paper to your audience. Tell them you can cut a hole in the paper that is large enough to walk through.
Step 2. Fold the paper in half lengthwise (Fig. 1).
Step 3. With scissors, make slashes on the paper. Note that there are seven cuts on the folded side and six cuts on the open side (Fig. 2).
Step 4. Cut from the first to the last slash along the fold (Fig. 3).
Step 5. Pull in opposite directions. Be careful not to rip the paper.
Step 6. Step through the paper with a big grin!

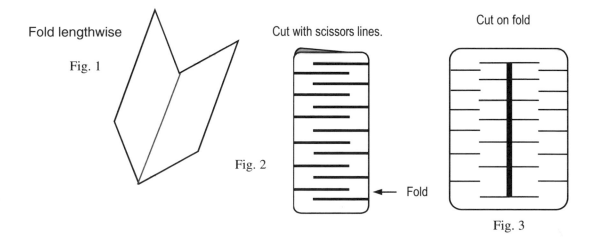

Fold lengthwise

Fig. 1

Cut with scissors lines.

Fig. 2

← Fold

Cut on fold

Fig. 3

Presto Paper Balls

Preview: Paper balls reappear in the spectator's hand.

Requirements: Four two-inch square pieces of tissue paper.

Preparation: Roll one of the papers into a ball, and hold this in left hand *finger palm* position. Put the other papers on the table.

Do the Trick:

Step 1. Crumple the three pieces of tissue paper into three small balls. Count them aloud as you do, saying "one, two, three."

Step 2. Place two of the three balls in your left hand, secretly add the ball hidden in *finger palm* position to the left hand.

Step 3. Pick up the remaining ball from the table with your right hand. Pretend to place this in your pocket. Secretly keep this ball in *finger palm* position.

Step 4. Open your left hand, and drop the three balls onto the table. The third ball has magically appeared with the other two balls.

Step 5. Repeat steps two, three, and four.

Step 6. Now, pick up a ball with each hand. Place the left-hand ball into your right hand, along with the *finger-palmed* ball. You actually have three balls. The spectators think you have two balls. Hand a volunteer the balls of paper. Tel that person to squeeze the balls tightly.

Step 7. Take the ball from the table and put it into your pocket. Tell the volunteer to open his or her hand. All three balls come rolling out. Have fun!

Cotton Ball Vanish

Preview: A cotton ball disappears.

Requirements: A cotton ball.

Preparation: You must learn the *finger palm*.

Do the Trick:
Step 1. Pinch the cotton ball with your right thumb and first two fingers.
Step 2. From the top, begin to close your left hand over the cotton ball.
Step 3. With your right thumb, pull the cotton ball into right hand *finger palm* position. Continue to close left hand into a fist as you separate your hands.
Step 4. Open your left hand. The cotton ball has *vanished*.

Cotton Ball Routine

Preview: Cotton balls magically appear and disappear in spectator's hands.

Requirements: Four cotton balls.

Preparation: Learn the cotton ball vanish. Place the 4 cotton balls in your right jacket or pants pocket.

Do the Trick:

Step 1. Remove two cotton balls from your right pocket and place them on the table.

Step 2. Place one cotton ball into your left hand and perform the cotton ball vanish. The ball remains in your right hand finger palm position (Fig. 1).

Step 3. With your right hand pick up the second ball (you now have both balls in your right hand). Squeeze them together so they appear to be one.

Step 4. Place both the cotton balls in a spectator's hand. Tell this person to keep his/her hand, tightly closed until they are told to open it.

Step 5. Open your left hand to show that the ball has vanished.

Step 6. Ask the spectator to open his or her hand, magically, the second ball appears. Tell the spectator to place the two balls on the table.

Step 7. While the spectator is opening his or her hand, you reach into your right pocket, remove the third ball, and secretly finger palm the fourth ball.

Step 8. Openly show the third ball. Put it on the table in front of you.

Step 9. With your right hand, pick up the first two balls adding the ball in finger palm position to them. Place these two balls (really three) into the spectator's hand.

Step 10. Pick up the remaining ball. Show it to the audience, and place it into your pocket.

Step 11. Snap your fingers, have the spectator open his or her hand and the third ball magically reappears in the spectator's hand.

Fig. 1

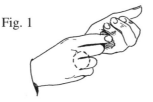

Brian's Bonus:

I have been performing a similar routine for many years. People always ask to see this trick. Practice it a lot, and you will have a real winner in your magical *repertoire*.

Cups & Balls

Preview: Cotton balls mysteriously go through the bottom of paper cups.

Requirements: Three small paper cups with *recessed* bottoms, four cotton balls.

Preparation: Place a cup right side up on the table. Place one of the cotton balls into this cup. Stack the other two cups into the first cup (Fig. 1). Place the three balls by the stacked cups on the table.

Do the Trick:
Step 1. With your left hand, pick up all three cups.
Step 2. Remove the top cup with your right hand and place it upside down on the table.
Step 3. Remove the bottom cup with your right hand and place it upside down, to the left of the first cup. This move must been done quickly as this cup contains the extra ball.
Step 4. Place the third cup upside down, to the left of the other two cups (Fig. 2). The cup with the ball under it should be in the middle.
Step 5. Pick up a cotton ball. Show it to your audience. Place this ball in the *recession* on the top of the center cup.
Step 6. Pick up the right cup with the right hand and the left cup with the left hand. Place these two cups on top of the middle cup.
Step 7. Snap your fingers. Lift all three cups together. It appears as though the ball went through the bottom of the cup.
Step 8. Hold the cups in upright position. Ball is now between the two top cups.
Step 9. With your right hand, remove the lower cup and place it upside down and to the right.
Step10. Remove the second cup (with the secret ball) flip it quickly and place it upside down to the left of the first cup and over the first ball. Place the cup in the left hand, upside down, to the left of the other two.
Step 11. Pick up the second ball and place it in the recession of the middle cup.
Step 12. Place the other two cups on the middle cup and snap your fingers. Like magic, the second ball has goes through the cup.
Step 13. Repeat steps 8 through 12.
Step 14. When finished with this trick, put the cups away so your spectators do not discover the extra ball.

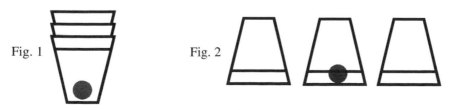

Fig. 1   Fig. 2

Glossary of Terms

Apparatus. Visible equipment used in a performance.

Buoyancy. Upward pressure exerted by a fluid.

Conceal. Hiding, covering, or keeping from sight.

Counter Clockwise. The direction opposite that of the rotation of clock hands.

Cutting. Removing cards from the top of a pack and replacing them on the bottom.

Deception. To mislead by a false appearance or statement.

Effect. What the overall appearance looks or feels like to the audience.

Execute. To carry out, perform or do.

Finger palm. A technique used to conceal an object behind fingers.

French Drop. Retaining an object in one hand while pretending to pass to another.

Gaze. To look steadily and intently.

Gimmick. Something used by the magician that the audience is not aware.

Glimpse. A very brief look or slight appearance.

Illusion. Deception by a false or misleading impression of reality.

Intently. Firmly fixed or directed.

Key Card. A known card, usually top or bottom card used to locate another.

Legerdemain. Sleight-of-hand.

Levitation. Rising or floating in the air.

Misdirection. The focus of attention that the magician controls through his actions.

Parallel. Extending in the same direction.

Preview. An earlier or advance view.

Palming. To conceal with or in the hand.

Patter. Rapid talk used to attract attention, entertain.

Prediction. To know in advance.

Production. An item that appears.

Recessed. Having an inner area or part.

Repertoire. All the tricks that you present.

Requirements. Something that is wanted or is needed.

Restoring. Bringing back, returning to original.

Retention. The act of keeping or holding onto.

Showmanship. Dramatic presentation.

Shuffle. To mix the cards.

Silk. Very thin cloth, also called silk scarf.

Simulates. To have the appearance of, copy.

Sleight-of-hand. Skill in feats requiring quick and clever movements of the hands.

Variation. To make differences between.

Vanish. To pass quickly from sight, disappear.

Appendix

About Magician Brian Irwin

For Brian Irwin, magic started when he was seven years old. He received a magic kit for his birthday, and the rest is history! Many people know Brian for his performances for Princess, Holland America, Costa, Royal Caribbean, and Premier cruise lines. Some know Brian from his tours to Japan and the Orient. Still others know Brian from his corporate events and product introductions. And a great number know Brian from his school assemblies. Brian says, "There is nothing like performing for a auditorium packed with children!"

Brian and his magic assistant wife, Lisa, live in Santa Maria, California, with their awesome assortment of critters and magic props. For more information, or to reserve a date on Brian's performance calendar call 1-800-549-3858.

Paul Fidler . . .on Brian Irwin

June 11, 1998

Dear Brian

Congratulations from Las Vegas, The Magic Capitol of the World, on your new and unique book of Magic. It is a fresh and clever idea and it supports a terrific cause, Research to find a cure for FOP.

Brian you know, I started performing magic tricks when I was only five years old. Today I am in my 25th year as a full time professional magician. I am currently contracted at the beautiful Las Vegas Excalibur Hotel, performing nightly until the year 2001.

Over the years I have known you, Brian, I have seen your first cruise ship performance, your first performance in Las Vegas, your first television show, and your first tour of Japan and the Orient. Now you have your first Book of Magic…you continually amaze me. Keep up the good work!

Your friend and "Brother in Magic"

Paul Fidler
'98

About Artist Anne Whitten

Born in Wheeling, West Virginia, Anne grew up amongst coal mines, steel mills, and country farms. Although resources were limited, her mother magically provided an on-going supply of crayons and paper—and they quickly became her friends.

Since moving to the California Central Coast, Anne has shared her gifts by creating masterpieces for her faithful coast-to-coast following and by teaching others. Anne works in acrylics. She used this media to create the spectacular front and back covers for *Out of the Hat, Children's Book of Magic*. Anne has been recognized with numerous art awards. She and her potter husband, Tony, reside in Santa Maria, California.

About Illustrator Anna Rubcic

Anna discovered she liked to draw when she was just three years old. Her skills at drawing what she saw were expanded by art classes in high school. Her degree in fashion design supported her favorite art focus of drawing people.

Anna has designed adult fashions and doll costumes, painted murals, and designed jewelry. She created the amazing drawings that illustrate the magic tricks in *Out of the Hat, Children's Book of Magic*. Anna has lived in Santa Maria most of her life.

Order Form

Out of the Hat
Children's Book of Magic

Name:_____ Phone:_____

Address:_____ City:_____ State:_____ ZIP:_____

Shipping/Handling: $4.50/book; additional @ $2.00. **Sales Tax:** CA residents add 7.75% to orders.

Please send_____books at $20.00 each $_____

Shipping/Handling $_____

Sales Tax (7.75%) $_____

TOTAL $_____

Payment: ❏ Check, payable to Boyce Press.

❏ Visa ❏ MasterCard

Card #:_____ Exp._____

Authorized
Signature:_____

☎ FAX ORDERS: (805) 934-1765

✉ MAIL ORDERS: Boyce Press
4869 S. Bradley #18B-208, Santa Maria, CA 93455

☎ QUESTIONS: 1-800-314-4556

Order Form

Out of the Hat
Children's Book of Magic

Name:_____ Phone:_____

Address:_____ City:_____ State:_____ ZIP:_____

Shipping/Handling: $4.50/book; additional @ $2.00. **Sales Tax:** CA residents add 7.75% to orders.

Please send_____books at $20.00 each $_____

Shipping/Handling $_____

Sales Tax (7.75%) $_____

TOTAL $_____

Payment: ❏ Check, payable to Boyce Press.

❏ Visa ❏ MasterCard

Card #:_____ Exp._____

Authorized
Signature:_____

☎ FAX ORDERS: (805) 934-1765

✉ MAIL ORDERS: Boyce Press
4869 S. Bradley #18B-208, Santa Maria, CA 93455

☎ QUESTIONS: 1-800-314-4556